Welcome to Brad King's Animal Coloring Books!

This book features elephants.

Brad is an exceptionally multi-talented teenage artist with autism living in south Florida. He has won numerous awards competing directly with other non-disabled peers and adults. Brad's art has been featured in calendars and art exhibits all over Florida. His art is ever evolving. Brad's love of the arts includes drawing, painting, sculpting, designing costumes and animation. He has been creating art since he was 5 years old. Brad is extremely prolific and most content when creating.

This series of coloring books has been a true passion for Brad. His love of animals lead him to wanting to save the wild animals throughout the world. This coloring book is a way for him to get his message out to everyone. Please see his hand written letter to hunters located at the end of this book.

To learn more about Brad King and his art please visit BradKingArt.com, www.etsy.com/shop/BradKingArt, also on Youtube.com search for BradKingArt.

Meet Brad . . . and please enjoy his Animal Coloring Book!

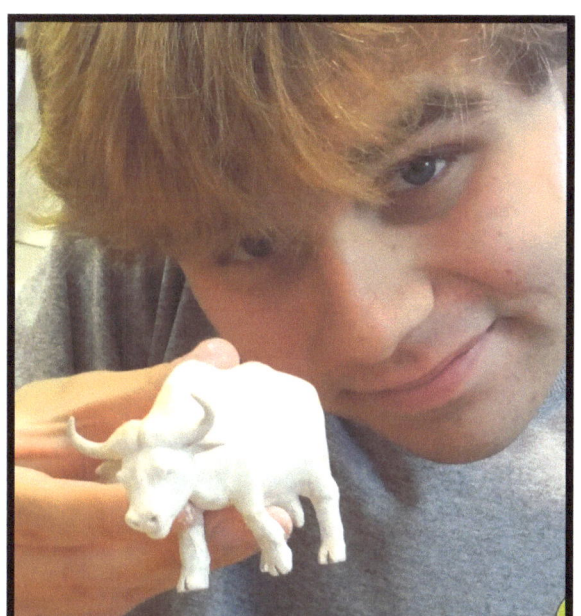

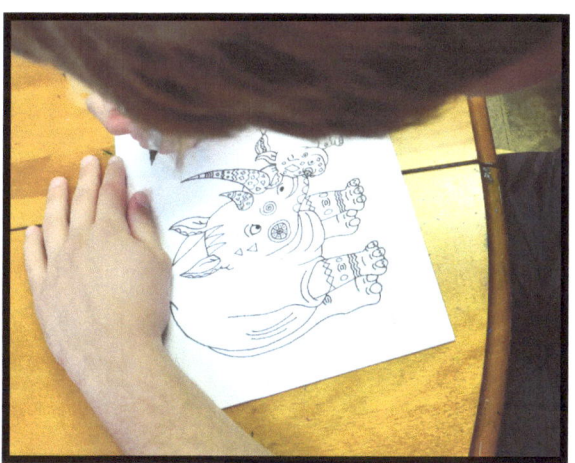

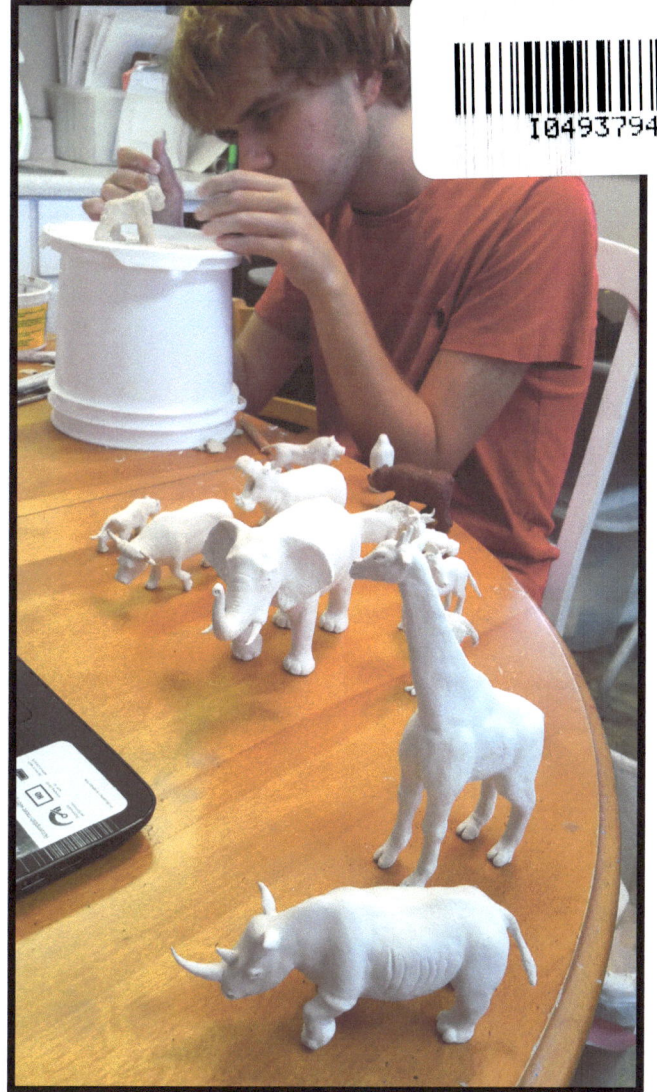

Elephants

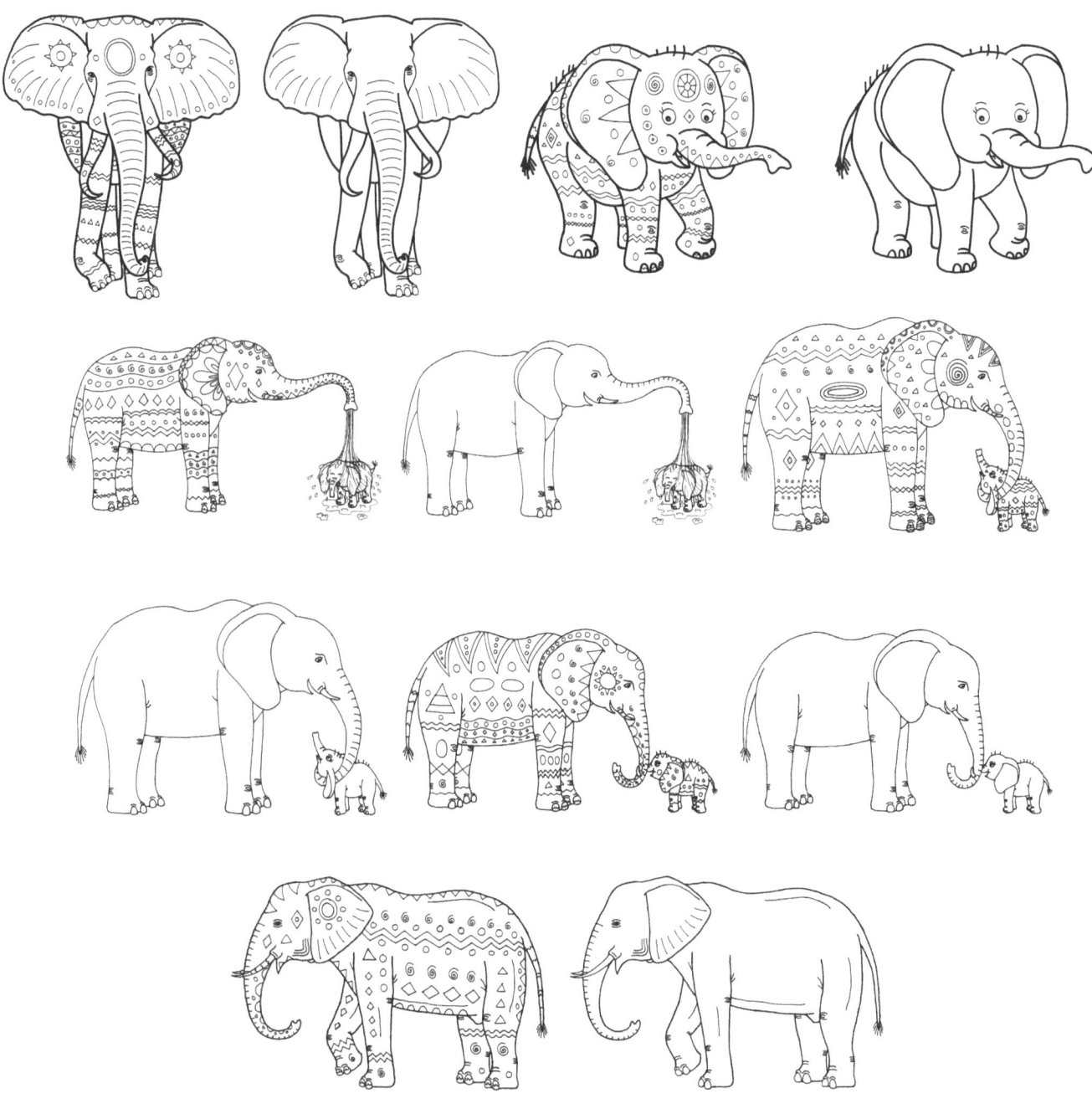

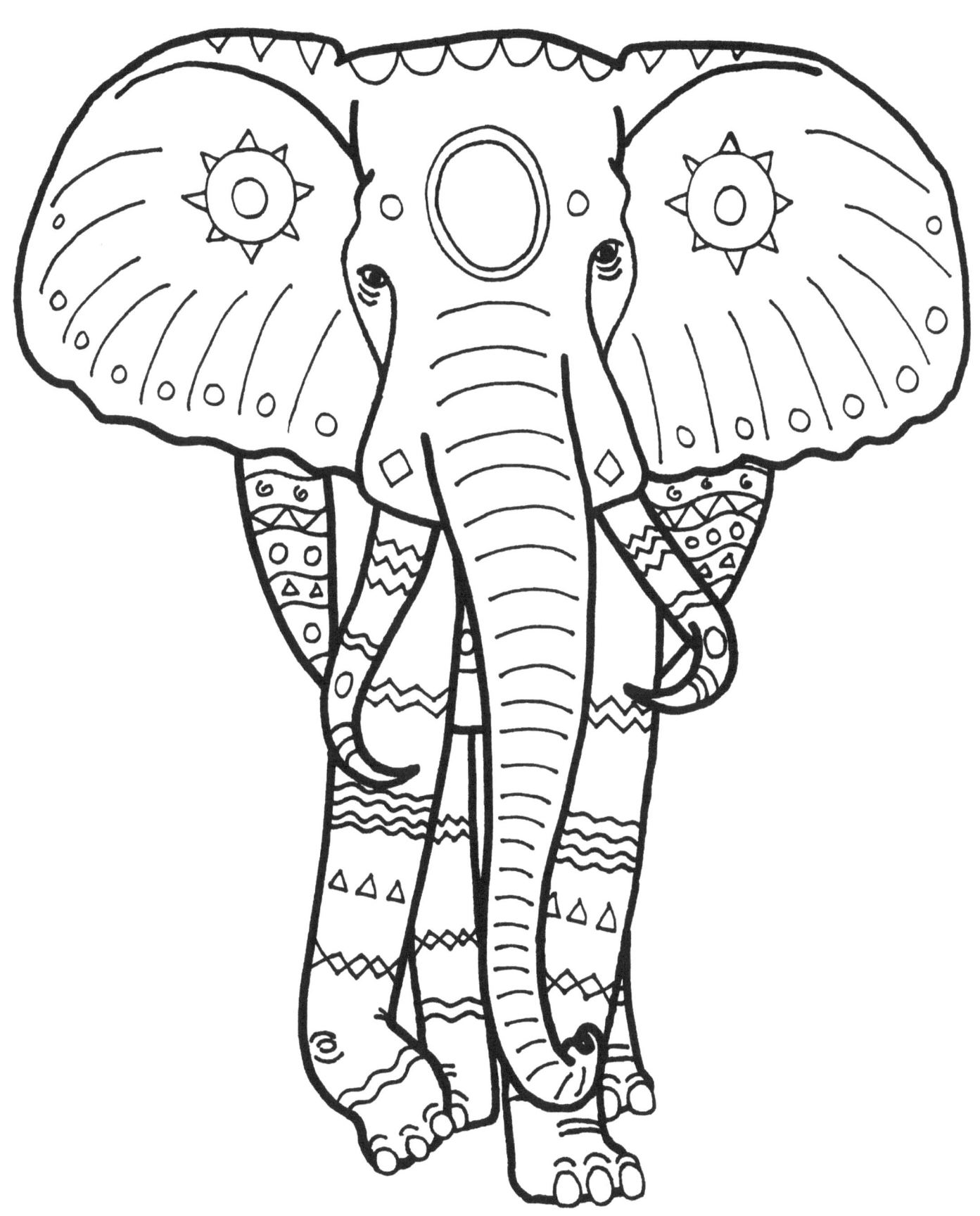

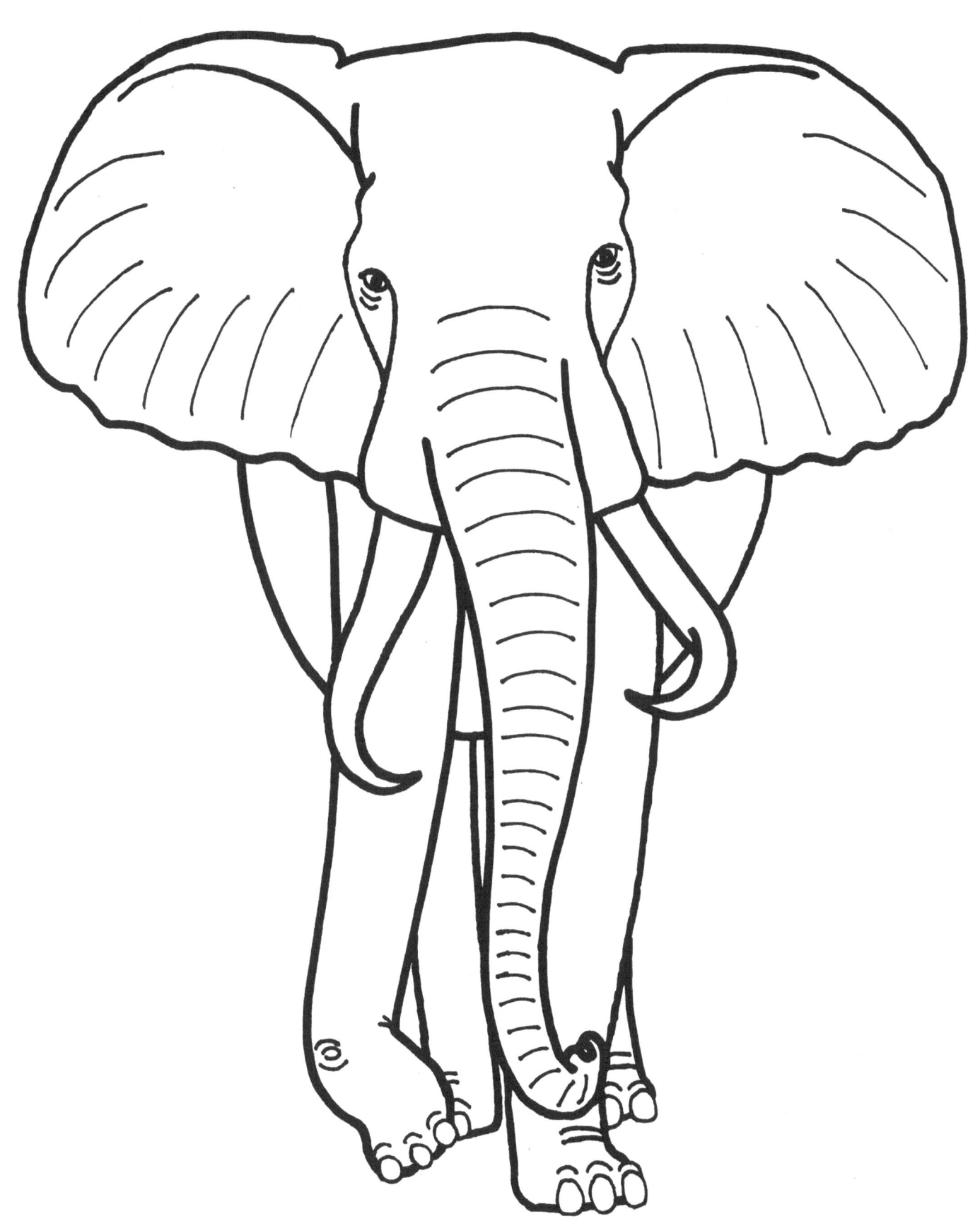

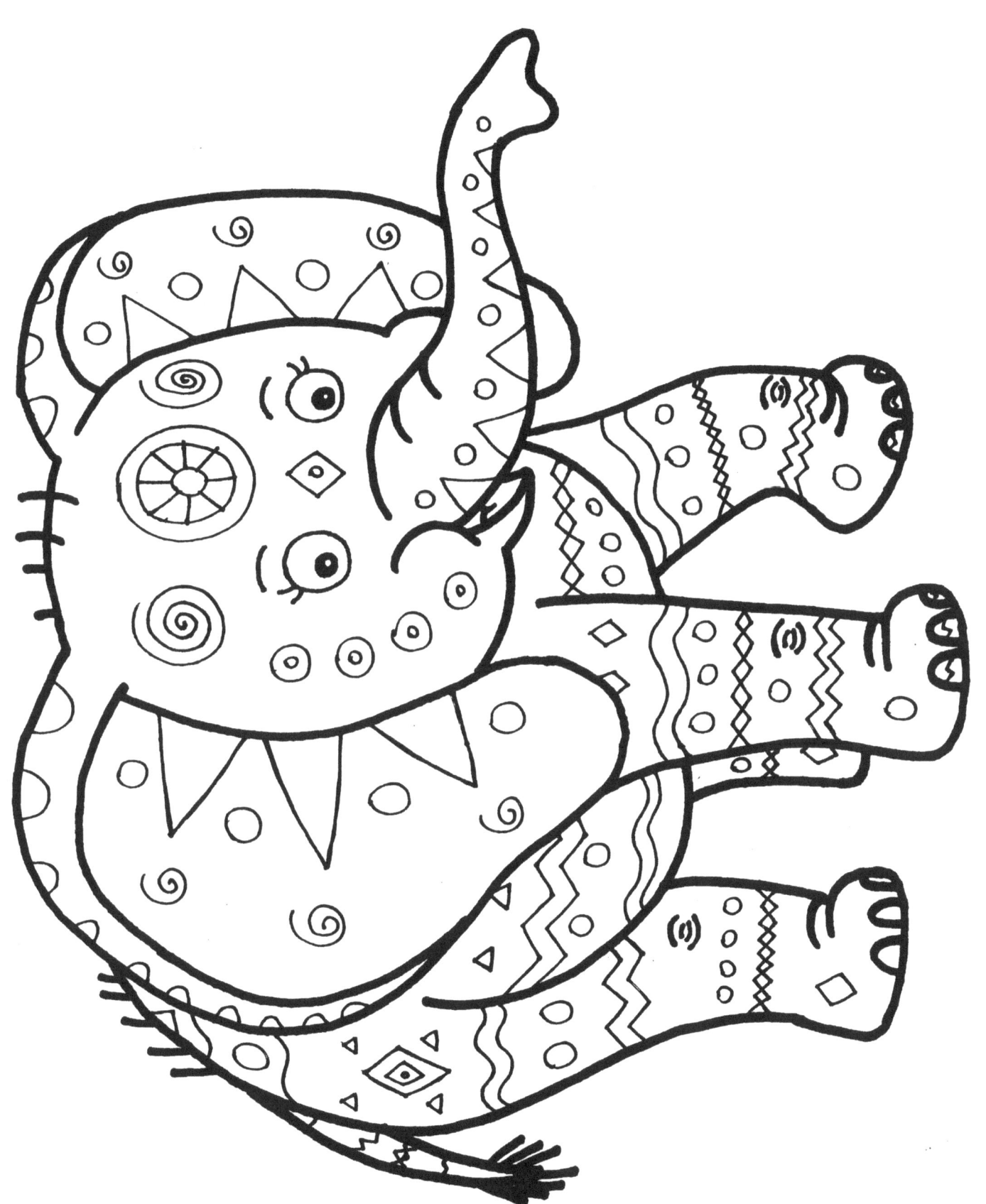

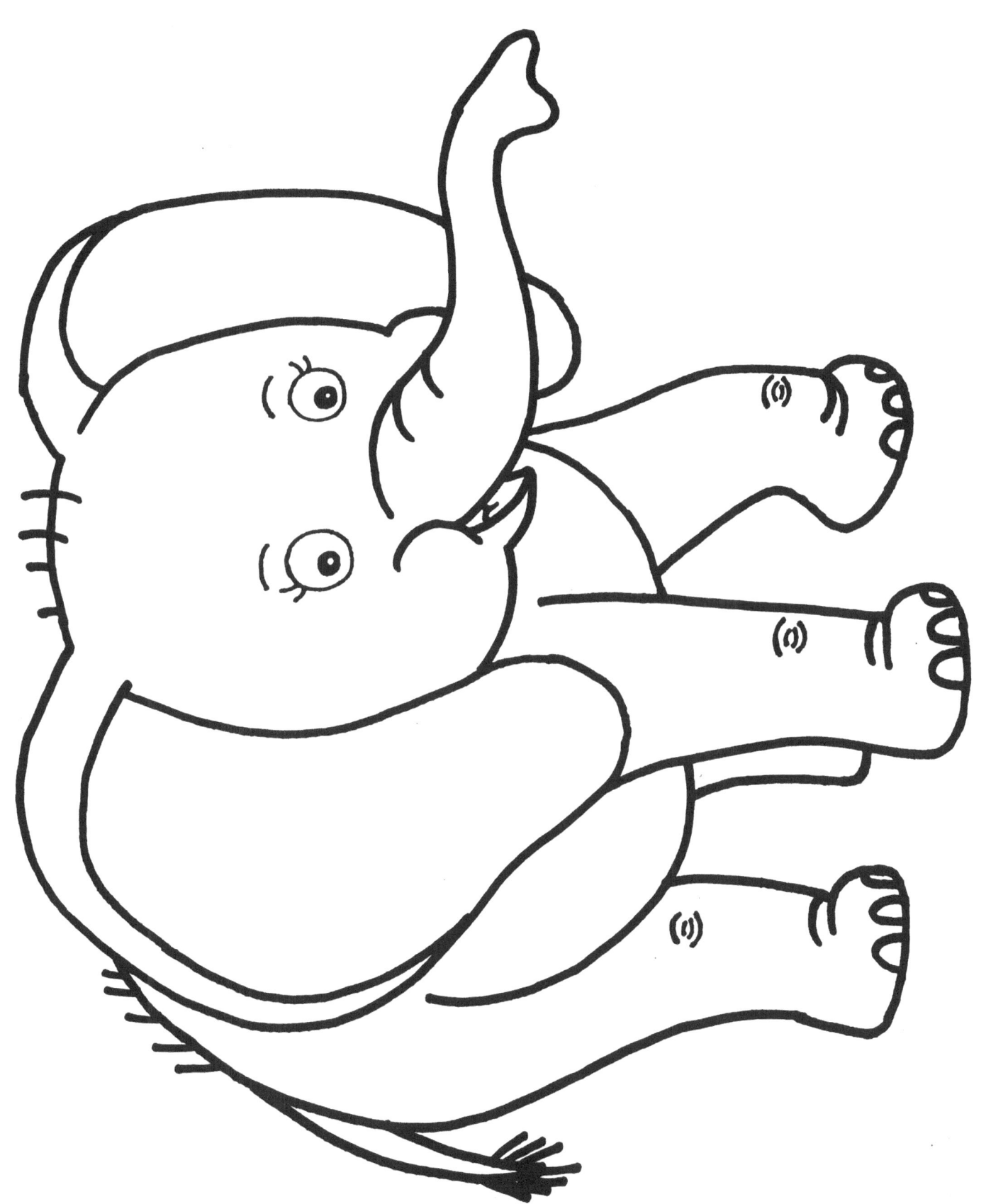

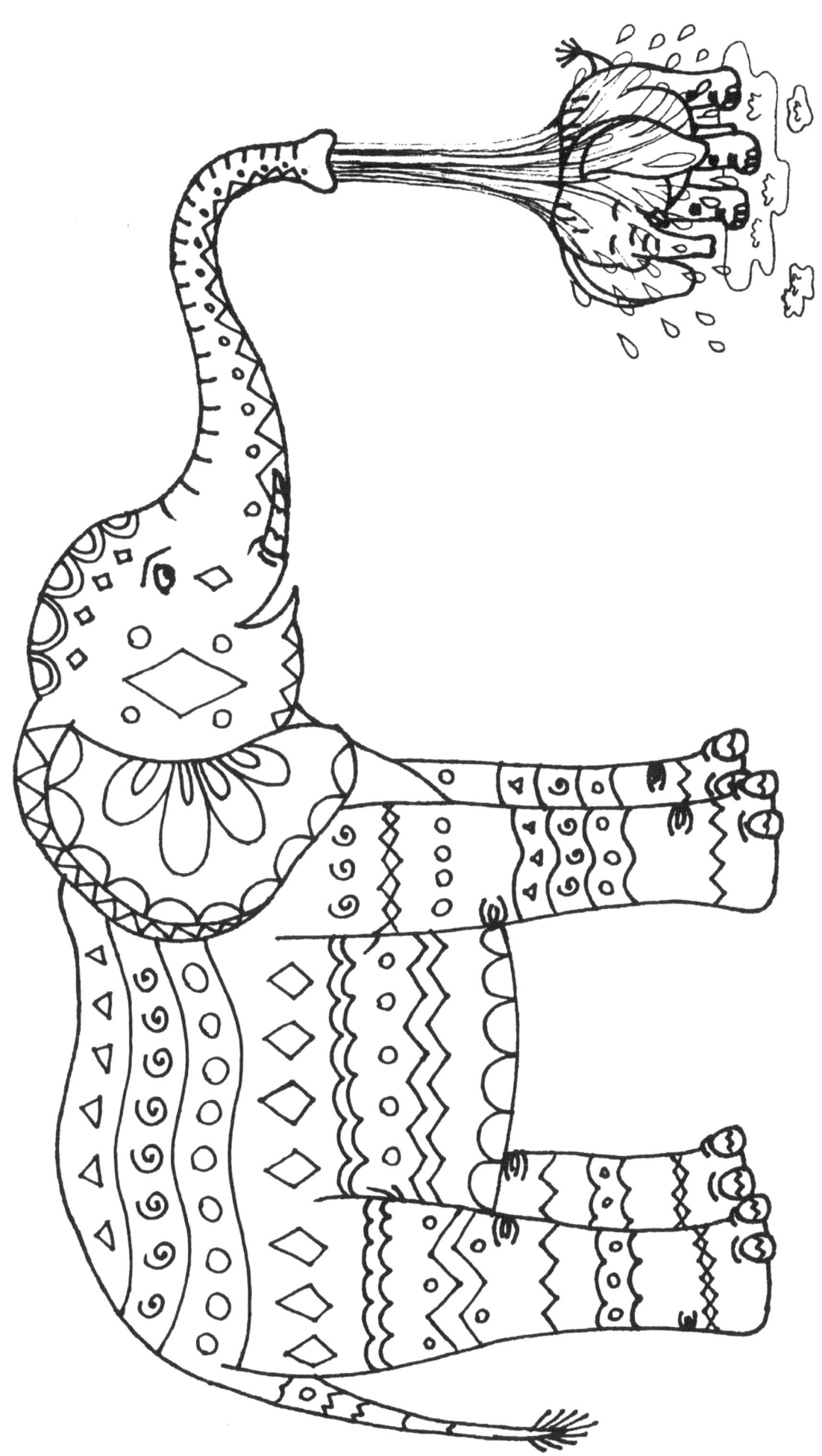

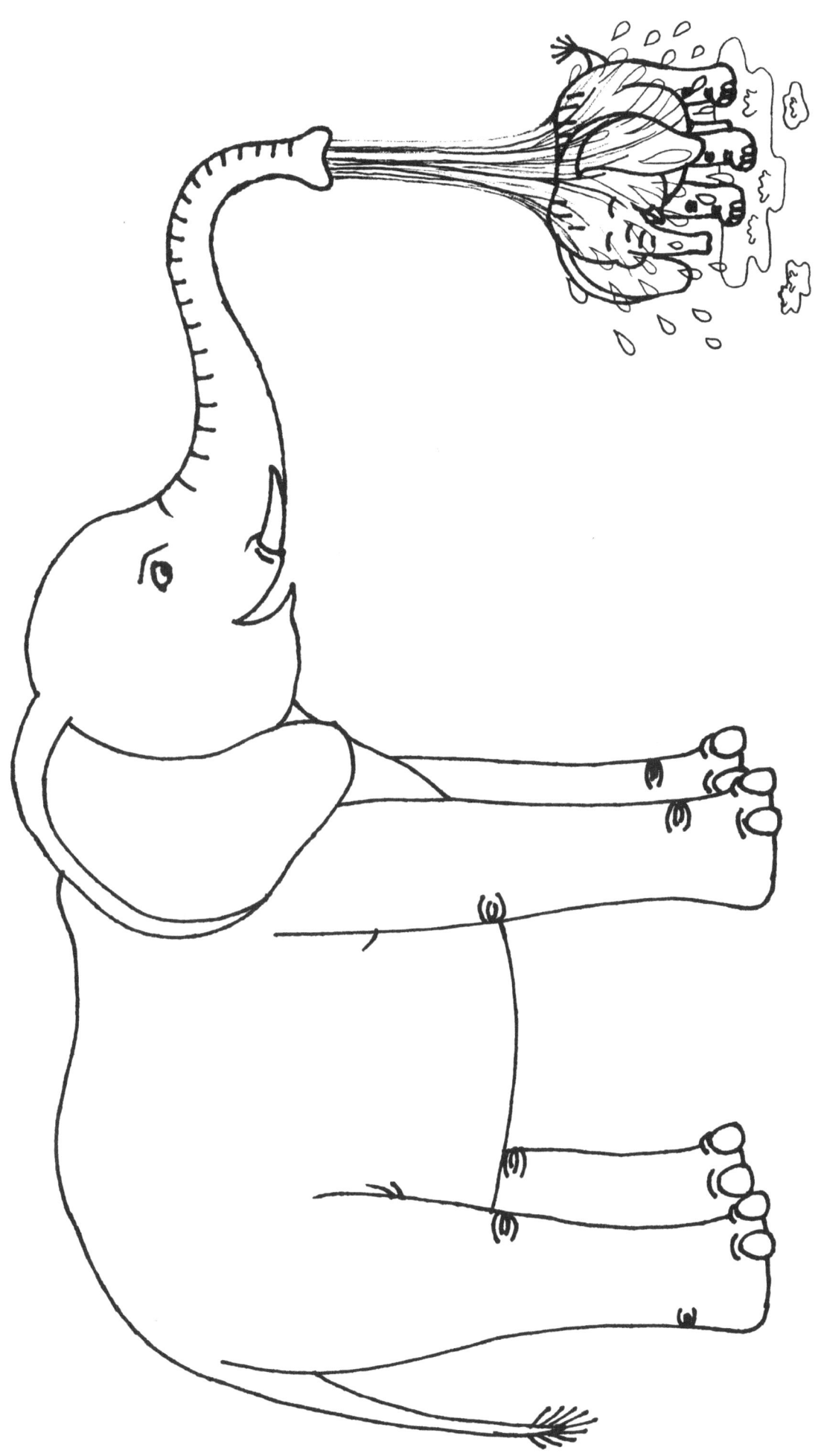

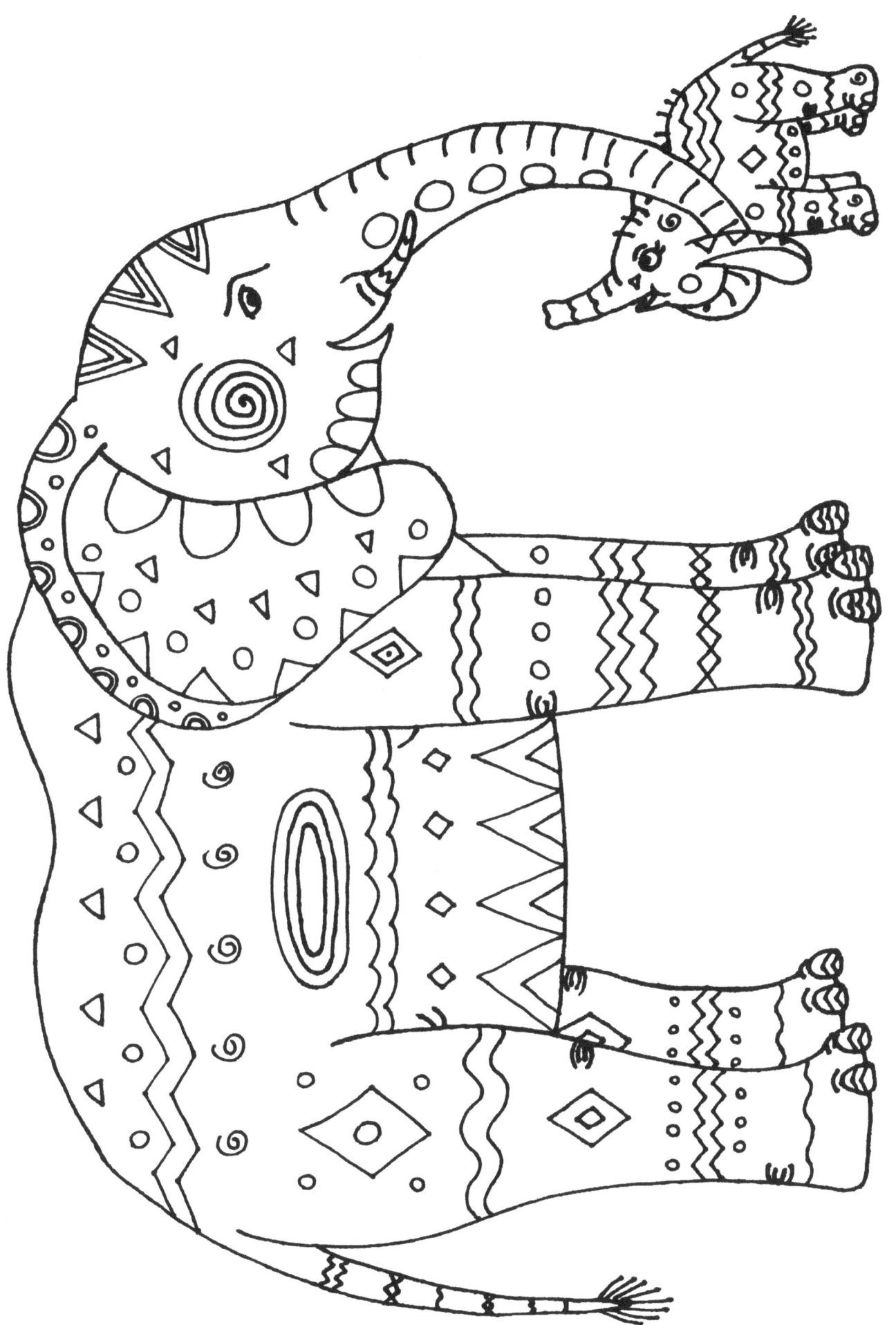

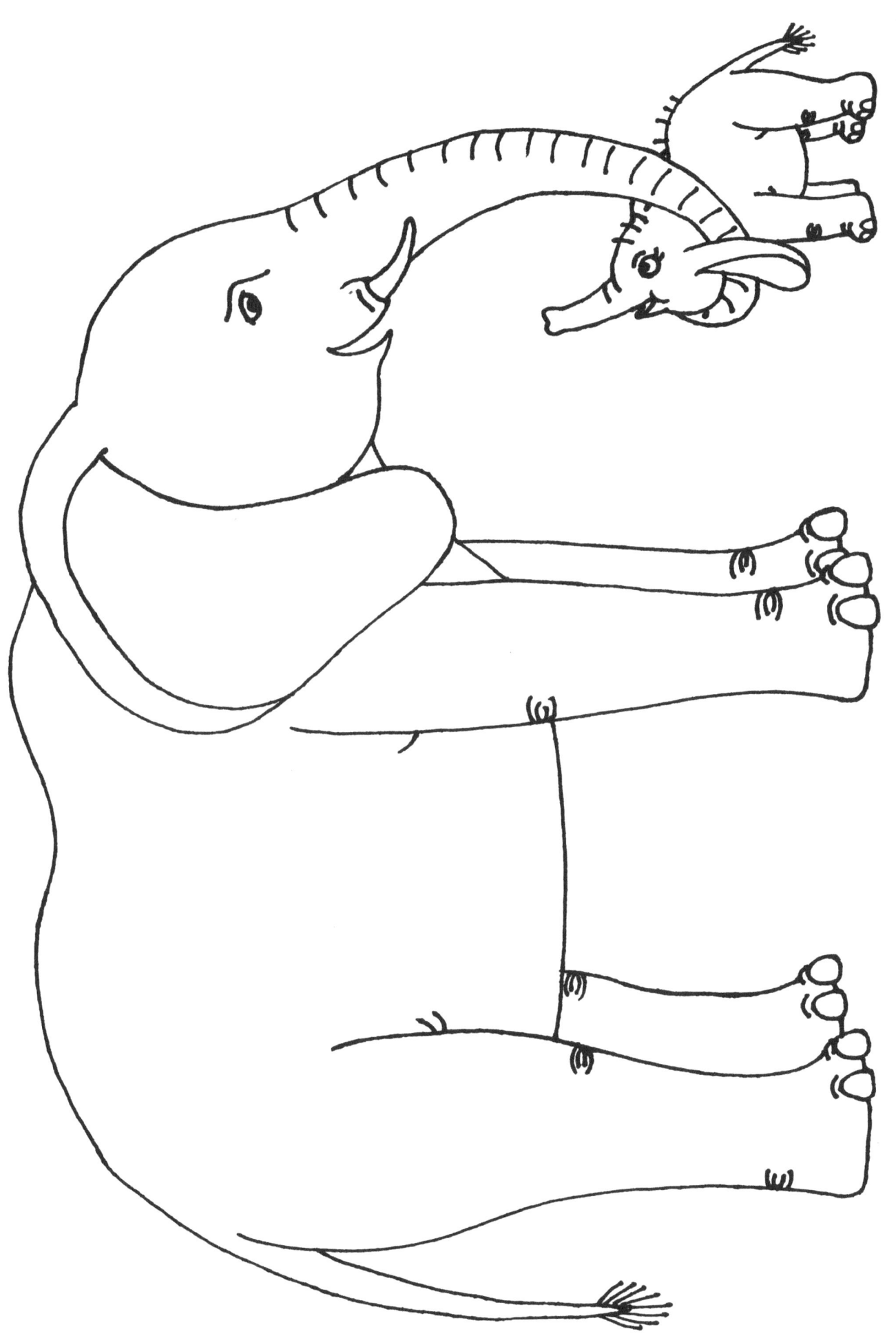

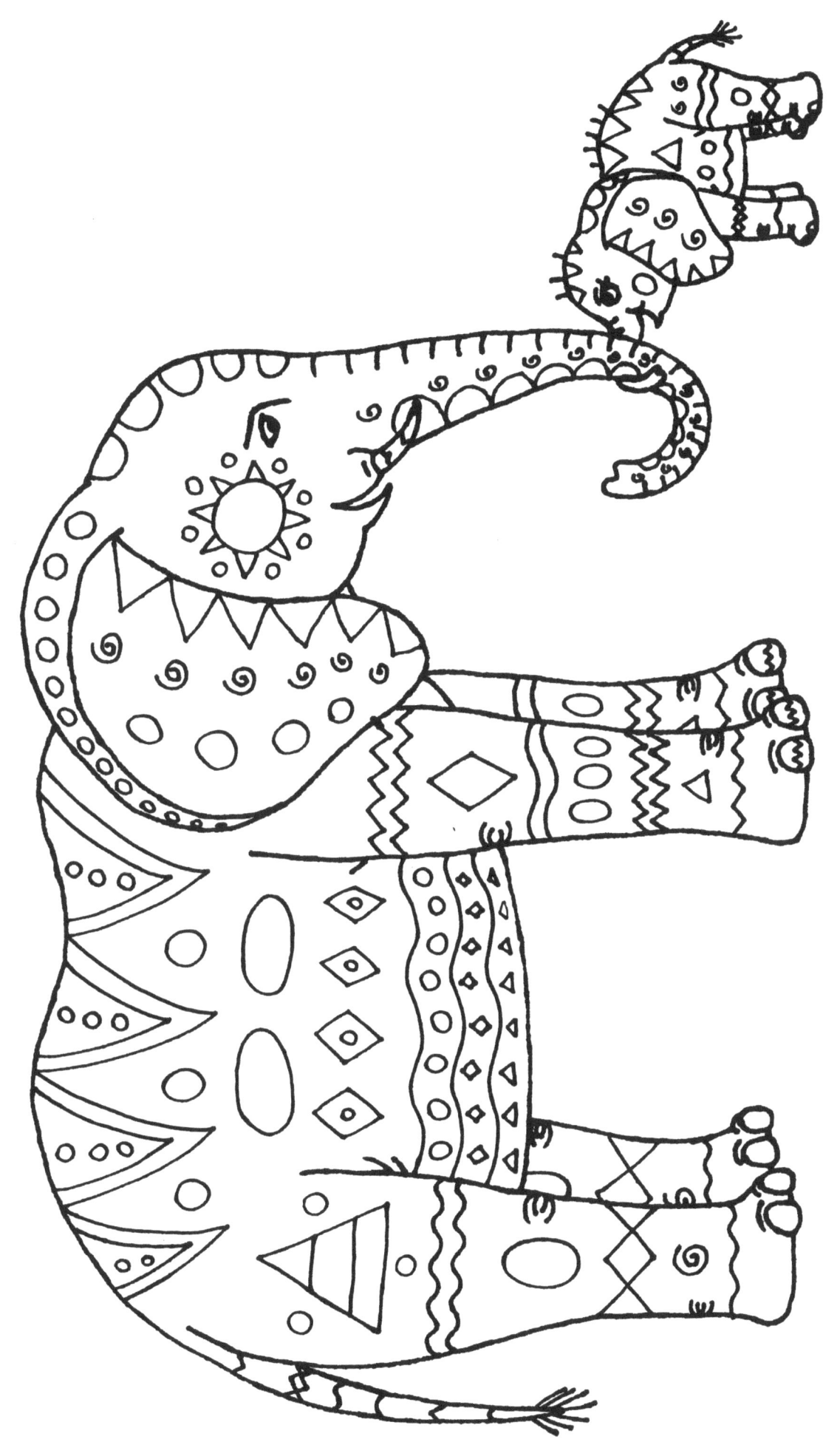

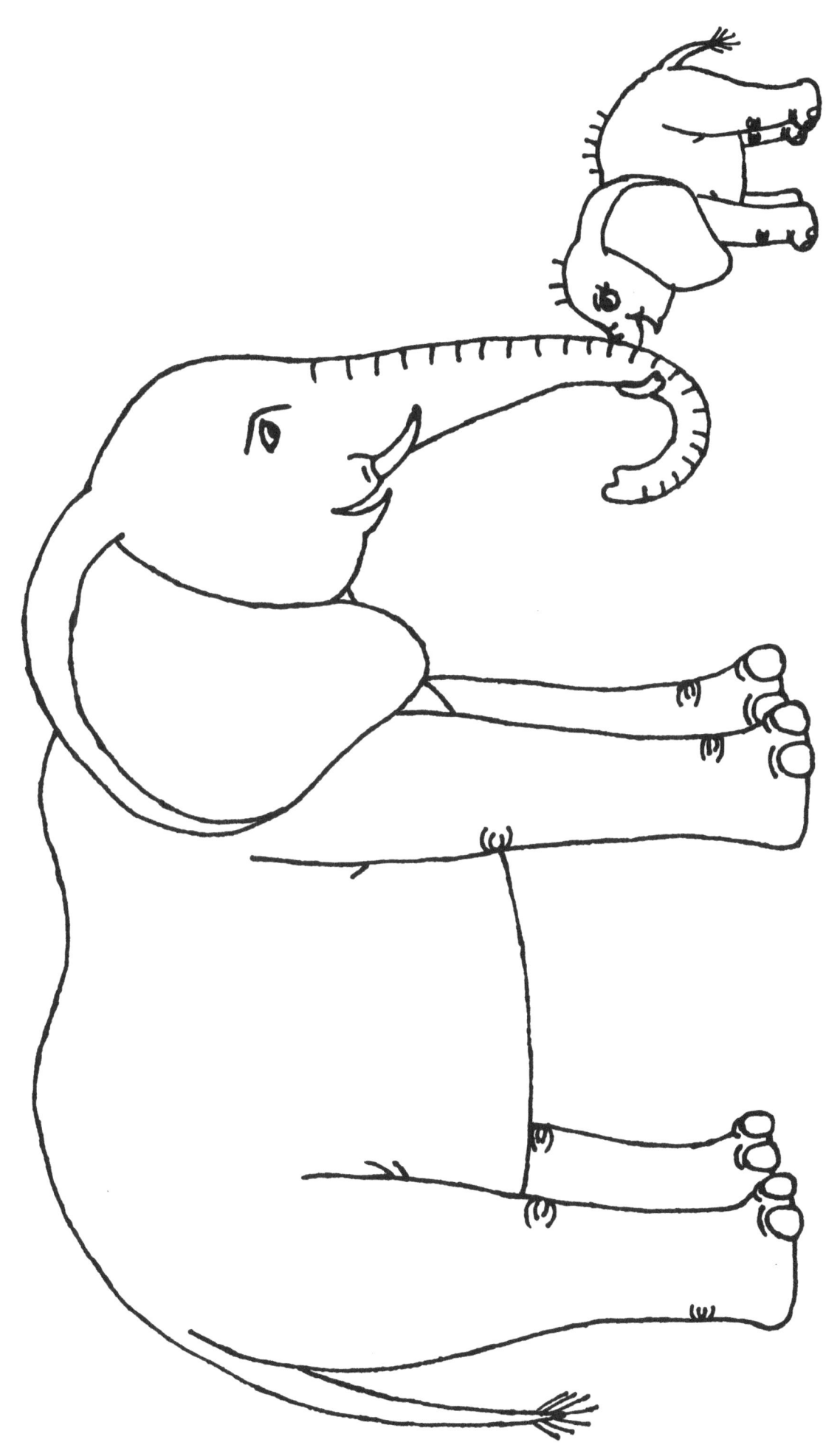

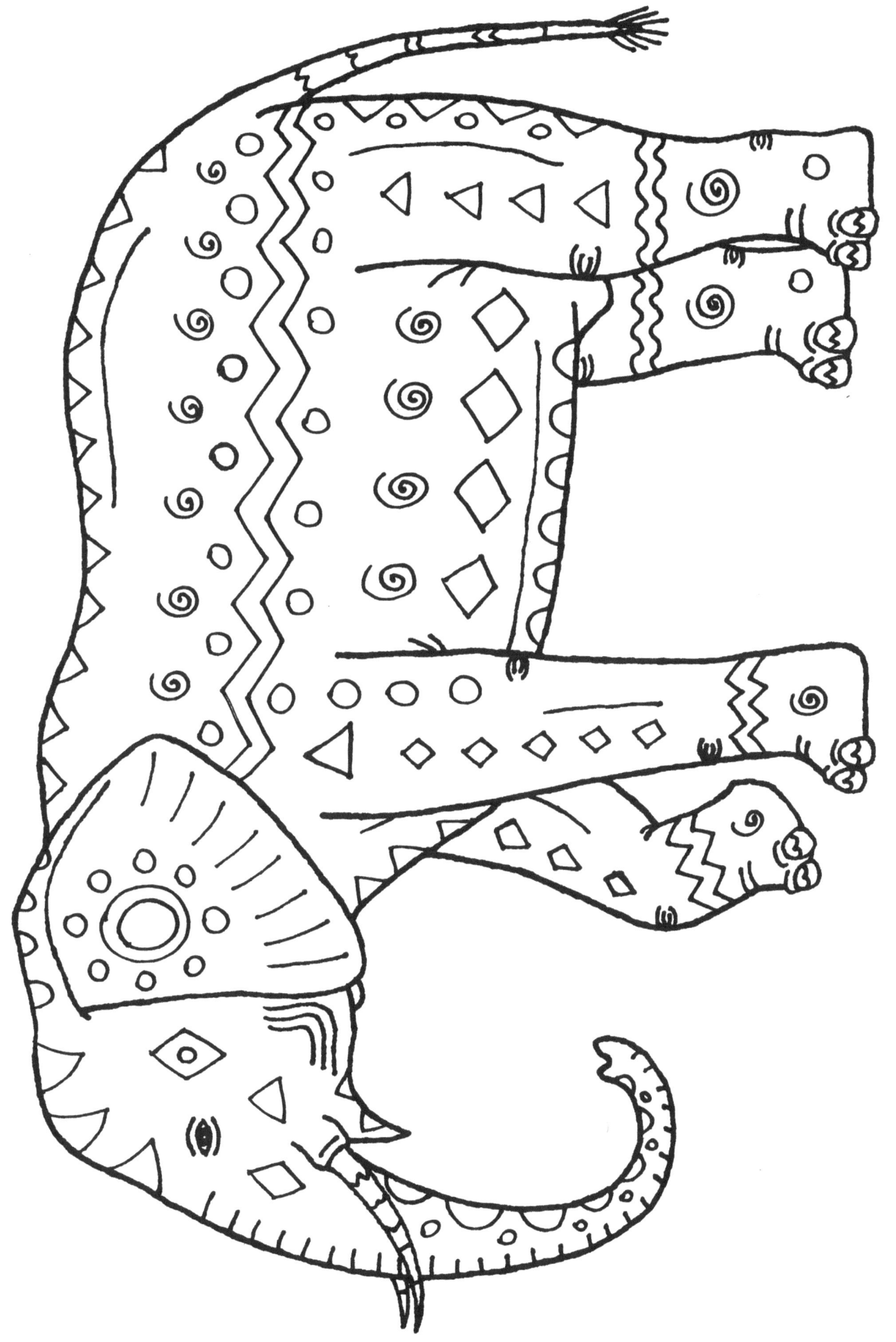

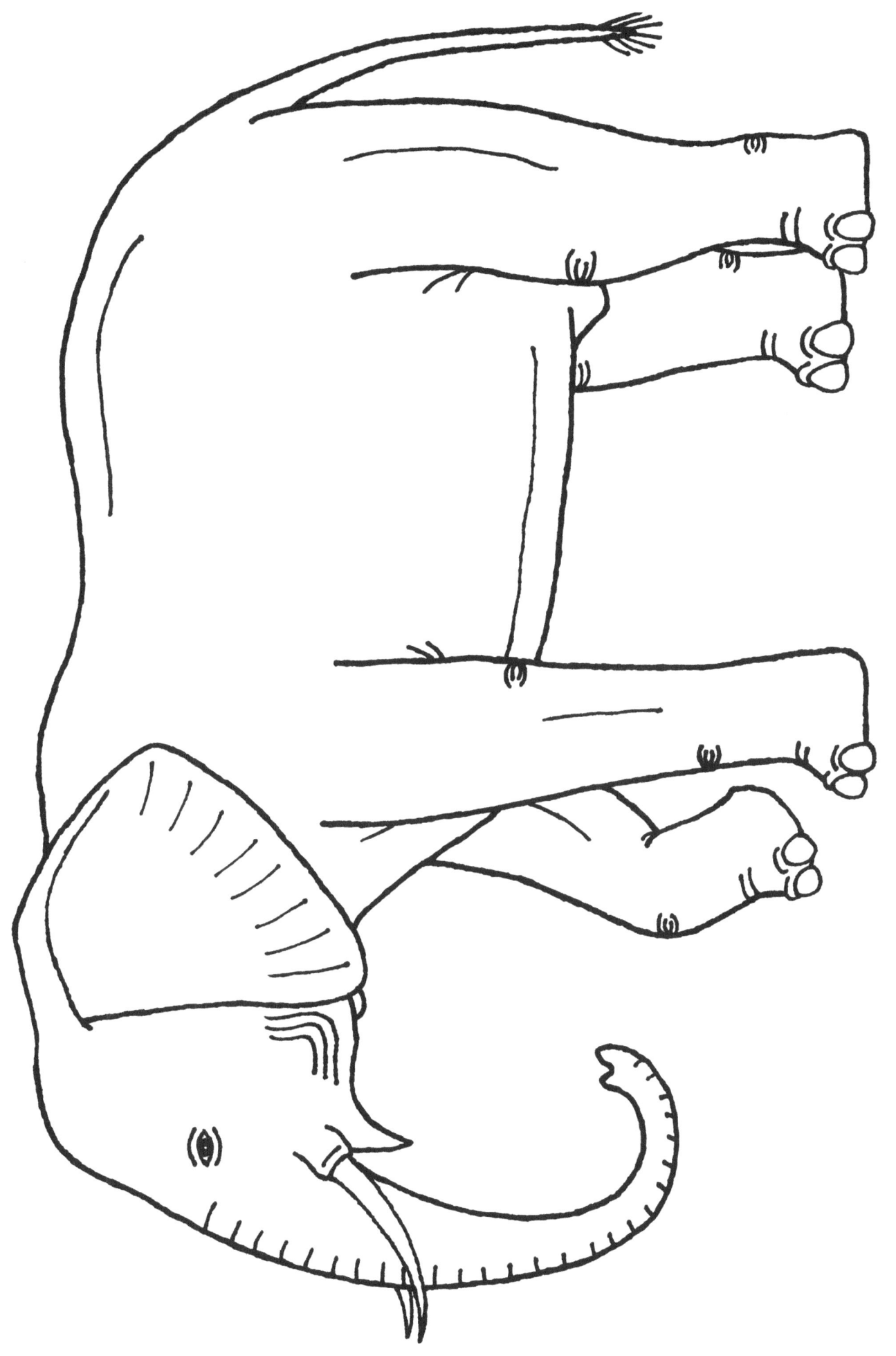

Please do not shoot all the animals in the wild. Like all the kinds of Rhinos, Elephants, Lions and other animals around the world. Do not shoot the animals in Africa, India, Asia, Australia, China, Russia, America, Canada, Mexico, Columbia, Antarctica, the Arctic and all other countries around the Earth. I want them all to Live.

from Brad King